# Review
# Prepare
# Execute
# Repeat

## Julia A. Royston

BK Royston Publishing
Jeffersonville, IN 47131
http://www.bkroystonpublishing.com
bkroystonpublishing@gmail.com

© Copyright 2026

All Rights Reserved. No part of this book may be reproduced, stored in a retrieval system, or transmitted by any means without the written permission of the author.

Cover Design: BK Royston Publishing
Cover Photo: Jonathan Snorten

ISBN-13: 978-1-967282-88-3

Printed in the United States of America

# Dedication

**All business owners everywhere.**

# Table of Contents

| | |
|---|---|
| Dedication | iii |
| Introduction | ix |
| **Phase 1 - Personal and Professional Branding** | **1** |
| Review Your Bio | 3 |
| Review Your Resume | 15 |
| Professional Photos | 19 |
| Professional Graphics | 23 |
| Create a One Sheet | 27 |
| **Phase 2 - Digital Presence and Infrastructure** | **33** |
| Review Your Website or Landing Page | 35 |
| Review or Create You Online Store | 39 |
| Review Your Social Media | 43 |

| | |
|---|---|
| Evaluate Your Technology | 47 |
| Review Equipment | 51 |
| **Phase 3 - Administrative and Financial Management** | **55** |
| Email and List Clean-Up | 57 |
| Review Taxes Procedures | 61 |
| Know Your Numbers | 65 |
| Contract and Agreement Review | 69 |
| **Phase 4 - Sales, Marketing, and Relationship Building** | **73** |
| Review Follow-Up System | 75 |
| Offering and Inventory Review | 81 |
| Funnel and Access Systems | 87 |
| Testimonials and Receipts | 91 |
| Reciprocal Partnerships | 95 |
| **Phase 5 - Growth and Professional Development** | **99** |

| | |
|---|---|
| Mentor, Coaching and/or Consultant | 101 |
| Professional Development | 107 |
| New Product/Service Creation | 111 |
| Team Building | 115 |
| Mission and Boundary Check | 119 |
| About the Author | 127 |
| Other Books by This Author | 129 |

# Introduction

The start of a new year is the perfect time to evaluate your business trajectory. This guide provides 24+ critical actions to help you audit your systems, refresh your brand, and optimize your operations. These items are not listed in a specific chronological order; rather, they are grouped by topic and serve as a checklist for you to prioritize your goals, business and clients based on your specific business needs.

As a business owner of more than 18 years, I find having this list critical for my business and hope that it helps you with your business.

If you have questions as a follow-up from reviewing this book, let's have a conversation at www.talkwithroyston.com or visit the website, www.bookbusinessboss.com for more tools and resources.

# Phase 1
# Personal and Professional Branding

Before you can sell your products, you must ensure your personal brand is current and professional.

You may not think it makes a difference, but it does.

If you are just starting out, you might not think you have a 'brand'. But you do. You are the brand. Until your business has a reputation, the reputation rests with you.

Think about it. What does your reputation say about you?

When people meet you, you are the representative, marketing, promotion, sales, financial and CEO of your business, book and brand.

No matter where you are starting from—scratch, rebranding or just reviewing the past month, quarter and year—put your best foot forward.

Let's go!

# Review Your Bio

This is something that I do all throughout the year. I constantly update my bio. I use the bio for the back of my books, event applications for larger events and to apply to be a speaker at an event. I also have an even more abbreviated bio for the end of articles, in my magazines and on social media, in my biographical sketches.

If you have problems writing a bio, I have created three episodes of the Book Business Boss Podcast to help you. Click on the links below and enjoy.

https://www.buzzsprout.com/1311391/episodes/16540607

https://www.buzzsprout.com/1311391/episodes/16546191

https://www.buzzsprout.com/1311391/episodes/16546197

Also, use AI to help you shorten long bios if needed.

Keys for a good, short bio that can be used for an introduction, back of a book or other printed or online materials:

**2-4 descriptive words for what you do.**

For Example,

Julia Royston.

Author. Publisher. Speaker. Coach.

**Who you serve?**

I serve those who have written or want to write a book.

**A glimpse into your why**

It is my tag, "Helping You Get Your Message to the Masses and Turn Your Words into Wealth."

How people can contact you and connect with you?

Schedule a conversation at www.talkwithroyston.com

If you provide a free download, do that too.

www.connectwithroyston.com

Create a Short and Long Bio

**Short Bio**

For Example,

Julia Royston spends her days doing what she loves, writing, publishing, speaking about her why and motto, "Helping You Get Your Message to the Masses, Turn Your Words into Wealth and Be a Book Business Boss." Julia is the author of 150+ books, published 500+, recorded 3 music CDs and coached others to be published authors and business owners. She is the owner of five companies, a non-profit organization and the editor of the Book Business Boss Magazine.

To stay connected with Julia, visit www.juliaakroyston.com.

Social Media

Facebook, Instagram, LinkedIn, TikTok and Threads - @juliaaroyston

YouTube - @bkroystonpublishing @bookbusinessboss

**Full Length Bio – Locate on my website, www.juliaroyston.net – Shown here only as an example and only posted or submitted on that website.**

Julia Royston is an author, publishing and motivational speaker, born and raised in Louisville, KY. Julia is the oldest of 3 daughters in a Christian family and is married to Mr. Brian K. Royston. Julia earned a B.A. in Accounting, two Masters Degrees in Information Science and a doctorate in Religious Education from Bellarmine University, University of

Kentucky, Spalding University and Grace Bible College, Niles, OH, respectively. Julia is a retired public elementary school Computer Technology Teacher/Media Specialist and currently a full-time entrepreneur.

Julia has appeared on The Bobby Jones Presents New Artist Showcase and ministered with notables such as Bishop Jackie E. McCullough, Pastor Donnie McClurkin, Bishop Noel Jones, Bishop Tudor Bismarck, Myron Williams and Bishop Richard "Mr. Clean" White. In December 2004 and 2005, Julia toured Switzerland with the Voices of Gospel Concert Series of St. Stephens Baptist Church.

In 2002, Julia established For the Kingdom Ministries with the mission to "Build God's People to Build the Kingdom of God" through education, empowerment and encouragement through inspirational music, high quality materials and messages of hope. For more information about For the Kingdom Ministries, visit http://www.juliaroyston.net/for-the-kingdom-ministries/

Julia has been singing since she was eight years of age and to date has recorded several music projects including, "Joy in His Presence", "A New Season in Word and Song", "Hymns for Him", "For Your Glory Lord", Begin Again, in Fall of 2019 released a Christmas single, "Christmas Miracle" and a quartet, churchy inspired tune, "Build the House." To purchase any of Julia's music, visit www.juliaroystonstore.com

In 2008, BK Royston Publishing Company was established and released its first book titled, "All New Season in Word." To date, Julia Royston has written 150+ books. To purchase them, visit http://www.juliaroystonstore.com. She has published or coached more than 350+ authors with close to 500+ books available for sale Internationally. If you're ready to publish your book, schedule your free consultation at visit www.talkwithroyston.com.

In 2013, Julia Royston Enterprises was established to provide consulting services to businesses, ministries and other organizations, to help them move their organizations to the next level with the skill set that God had given.

In 2015, a second publishing company, Royal Media Publishing was established to provide an outlet for the authors with mainstream topics for a global audience. Royal Media Publishing is committed to publishing high quality manuscripts to bring to the forefront issues that touch every walk of society. For more information about Royal Media and Publishing, visit http://www.royalmediaandpublishing.com.

In 2016, after major thyroid surgery, Julia recorded her latest music CD, "Begin Again," with 9 original songs and 1 hymn, "Down at the Cross/Glory to His Name," which symbolized the recovery and victory throughout this process. To purchase the CD, visit http://www.juliaroystonstore.com.

In 2018, Julia established Royston Book Fairs for children's books for schools and other non-profit organization as a means for exposing great children's literature to new audiences and as a fundraiser for these same institutions. To purchase books for your child, personal enjoyment, schools and/or non-profit organization, visit http://www.roystonchildrenbookstore.com.

In 2019, Julia established the Book Business Bosses Author Community, to coach, train and assist authors to take their books to the next level of exposure and opportunity for marketing and promotion. For more information about the Book Business Bosses, visit http://www.bookbusinessboss.com. The Book Business Boss Magazine is published to give quality articles and information for future authors as well as promote the new released books from BK Royston Publishing and Royal Media and Publishing. To obtain the latest copy visit http://www.juliaroystonstore.com.

In November of 2019, Julia began hosting the "Live Your Best Life" Broadcast and Podcast. For the replays, visit http://liveyourbestlifewithroyston.com.

In 2022, the Book Business Boss Show was added to the Envision Radio line-up to air on Tuesdays at 10:30 a.m. EST. The Book Business Boss Show is designed to talk about Writing in Season 1, Publishing in Season 2, Promotion in Season 3 and the Book Business in Season 4. In Season 5, which will begin airing in 2026, the theme will be turning your Book into a Business as well as newly released books from Julia A Royston. Tune in on Tuesdays at 10:30 a.m. EST to talk about all things literary on the Book Business Boss Show on www.envision-radio.com where Praise Meets Talk 24/7.

2026 marks 18 years that BK Royston Publishing has been in business. Julia Royston continues to speak, empower and inspire people around the world to write, publish their books and to live the abundant life that is their Purpose and Destiny.

Keep up with Julia on Social Media by following or liking her pages on Facebook, Instagram, LinkedIn, TikTok and Threads @juliaaroyston | YouTube @bkroystonpublishing and @bookbusinessboss

# Reflection for Review

## Reflection for Review

# Review Your Resume

Even as an established business owner, contracts often require a current resume. Maintain various versions tailored to different services (e.g., educator, consultant, practitioner).

I have multiple resumes for the various roles and positions that I've held. I have a resume for my business and the services that I provide. I have a resume for when I was an educator, but it contains my experience and the places where I taught.

I have a resume as a consultant for those who wish to contact companies or people I have consulted with. I have a resume as a coach as well as a resume for where I participated in ministry as a praise and worship leader in various churches and ministry.

Even though I'm from retired from teaching and in business full time, I keep my resumes current, for that just-in-case opportunity. Remember, the skills that you have from a job, non-profit, ministry or other organization are skills that can never be taken away. Don't diminish any of your abilities because they can all pay off. Let's go!

Keys for a good resume.

Be specific.

Write for the position that you are applying for.

Write in active voice, i.e. what did you do? What can you do now? What did you do that helped progress or upgrade the company or organization that you worked for? What skills can you offer a company right now?

Make sure that your contact information is current and your work history can be verified.

Notify your references.

Make sure your resume is free of errors.

# Reflection for Review

## Reflection for Review

# Professional Photos

Ensure you have high-quality headshots and full-body shots that look like you *now*.

Now, I'm pretty obsessive about high-quality headshots. I have professional photos done every time I really change my hair because I want people to see how I look now and not how I looked back then. I have natural hair texture so I had new pictures because sometimes I wore a weave or put on a wig in my headshots and in-person. I take new pictures so people can see what I will look in-person now.

Make sure you have a professional photo done and you may have to have touchups done to them, depending on how well your makeup is done or blemishes, etc. There are filters that can help you as well.

Bathroom selfies are okay when you just, *I just thought I was cute tonight and I look good so I took a picture of myself.* But if you're submitting a headshot for coaching or to speak at an event, business cards, postcards, etc., you need a professional headshot done.

Now, AI can do a lot with headshots and professional photos, but they need to look natural and not too glammed up so people are still able to recognize you.

You get what you pay for, and if you pay for it, it should give you a return on your investment. If you don't have a critical eye, have a friend take a look to determine if it is professional or not.

A professional headshot can and will make the difference.

# Reflection for Review

## Reflection for Review

# Professional Graphics

Your short bio, photos and contact information are all connected to and an essential part of your professional graphics. Who are you? What do you look like? How can people find you to work with you?

You have the basics down, so next, are the professional graphics. The layout, colors, font and your images will cause some people to be attracted you. Then, they want to find out more information. Next, they go to your website, landing page or bio link site. They have your contact information on your graphics, they, hopefully, will reach out, contact you and the goal is to do business with you.

How do you get professional graphics done? I am so glad that you asked. I do a whole lot of my graphics myself, using CANVA. If you need help, I have an Instant Access Course available at www.juliaroystonstore.com all ready and prepared for you to take anywhere and anytime.

Canva is truly my friend. They have the templates to guide you and help you on your business owner journey. If I need a graphic for a next level project, I have a professional graphic designer do it. If you need help, reach out to me.

My suggestion is that you should create a set of templates in Canva with your headshot and quotes from your work, to use for consistent sales, branding and social media posting throughout the year.

# Reflection for Review

# Reflection for Review

# Create a One Sheet

Develop a single-page document containing your headshot, short bio, contact info, and core services for quick distribution to potential clients, partners and networks.

Essential parts of a one sheet are:

Headshot

Short bio

Testimonials from Customers/Clients

Services offered

Contact information

Tag Lines

Specific Speaking Topics

New Products/Books

If you need help creating or being advised about a one sheet, reach out.

# Examples of One Sheets

# Reflection for Review

## Reflection for Review

# Phase 2
# Digital Presence and Infrastructure

The world is literally online, especially on their phones. In business, you need to be accessible via all forms of technology. Your phone, mobile device and social media are essential places that you need to have a digital presence.

I love in-person as much as the next person, but you need have to have a digital presence and headquarter somewhere on the Internet.

# Review Your Website or Landing Page

Ensure you have an internet-accessed place for people to find you. Your "digital storefront or headquarters" must be accessible and easy to navigate.

Do you have internet real estate? Do you have a place where you are that is your headquarters for your business or organization? I'm not going to say I don't necessarily trust you if you don't have a website, but it helps, and if I can't find you online, I may be reluctant to do business with you. Having an internet site or website helps to verify, certify and validify you.

Now, if you're an author, you should at least have an author central page. Go to www.author.amazon.com to establish an author central for those of you who have published books.

Keys to updating your website:

Does the copyright at the bottom or the footer say 2020 on it or does it say the current year?

What's available on your website, your bio, books available, merchandise or a link to an online store? Do you have an online store?

What's coming up next?

What are you, or what are you on the horizon, doing? Are you writing something? Are you producing something? Are you changing something? Are you rebranding something?

Then your website needs to reflect it.

If a full website is too much, utilize a landing page or bio link site (like Linktree or solo.to) Even if you haven't created a full website, do you have a Linktree or solo.to site or an about.me one page site? If not, check out my bio link site at www.juliaakroyston.com.

We are clearly in the Digital, Online and Virtual Space; you need a website to sell online and make money while you sleep.

## Reflection for Review

# Review or Create You Online Store

In a virtual economy, having an e-commerce presence (Shopify, Etsy, etc.) is vital to ensure you can make money even if in-person events are unavailable. Also, this is one prime way that you can make money while you sleep.

Marketing and promotion of your online store is taking place and people literally around the world can purchase what you have to offer. The key is that you have to have products or services to offer, the store up, running, current, available and being promoted so that people can find it.

People need at least 15-20 times or opportunities to see what you have to offer. One time is not going to cut it. Once a month is not going to cut it, either. Text, a graphic, short video, long video and live stream are all going to be necessary and consistent for people to know who you are, what you offer, know how to access you and THEN consider whether they are going to purchase or not.

The e-commerce stores are wonderful, but once you get more traction, get a bigger audience and have more to offer, consider putting the online store, website and email communication and marketing system all together.

It's in the future if you are starting out, but plan for it and prepare for it. In the meantime, you can't be profitable without products. These products can't make you profit unless you promote.

Check out my ecommerce store at www.juliaroystonstore.com or www.roystonchildrenbookstore.com.

Need help, reach out.

# Reflection for Review

# Reflection for Review

# Review Your Social Media

Evaluate your handles and profile pictures on all of your social media platforms. Ensure your branding is professional—consider if a "personal" handle still matches your business goals.

Where are you on social media? Is your ideal client there on that platform? Are you seeking to sell to women, men, young people or older adults?

Do you have your contact information listed? Do you have a shortened biographical information listed to give a newcomer some insight into who you are and what you offer?

When posting, know that the amount of text, who sees your posts and the changes that the social media platform allows, change frequently. Be sure to log in and double check.

Do you have a new email?

Do you have a new website?

Be sure to update the bio info on your social media, especially if you are in business. People are trying to find you and do business with you but can't because you don't help them find you.

How often do you post? Once a day, week, month, quarter or hardly ever?

What is your handle?

Does your business branding match with how you are seen on the platform or not? If not, consider establishing a separate page for business from personal if they do not complement each other at all.

Find me on social media for hints and ideas.

Social Media

Facebook, Instagram, LinkedIn, TikTok and Threads - @juliaaroyston

YouTube - @bkroystonpublishing @bookbusinessboss

# Reflection for Review

## Reflection for Review

# Evaluate Your Technology

You can run much of a business from a quality smartphone, but you must plan for hardware upgrades (laptops, storage, etc.) every few years.

Does your laptop run slow? Do you work on the road? Consider having a laptop as well as a desktop computer at home. A mobile device such as an iPad or other tablet could be essential as well.

How many pictures can you store or even download?

When was the last time you purchased a smartphone?

I have my emails, send invoices, check social media, respond to text messages, make and receive electronic payments and can create notes and/or documents right through my phone. It is essential that I have the capability to be able to continue to run and do business straight through my phones. I travel to large trade shows, speak and sell from my phone.

A new phone is not necessary ever single year, but if it has been 5 years, start saving and prepare to upgrade your phone for better service, storage and performance.

Technology is here to stay. With the added bonus of the capabilities of AI, you need to make sure that you have the technology to handle all of the new possibilities, opportunities and information that is quickly going to be coming your way.

Need help, reach out or visit www.juliaroystonstore.com to purchase the book, "Doing business in the digital, online and virtual space."

# Reflection for Review

## Reflection for Review

# Review Equipment

Review your equipment. When I started in business, I sang and would carry a few CDs down in a large tote. I would have a yellow note pad to write down any new contacts or people to follow-up with for new opportunities to sing. I really didn't have enough product to need anything else.

Now, 150 books, tents, tables, chairs, stands, retractable banners, business cards, postcards, brochures, etc. require more equipment. I now have 3 rolling carts, large industrial-sized containers and other sturdy equipment to carry very heavy books and other promotional materials.

I had to save, re-invest, plan and prepare for these purchases. I didn't always have the funding or the savings for these types of purchases. But when the budget could afford it, I purchased these items at the best price ever. My first rolling cart was $200 but the demand for carts has caused the pricing to go down for a small cart from $50-$75 and for a large cart around $100.

Do you need a retractable banner to see your basic information and promote your business?

Do you have a tablecloth or runner over the table that promotes your business with the contact information on it? I started with a black king-sized sheet and then regular table cloths from the grocery story and then a proper, fitted table cover and promotional runner.

One of the more recent things that I have invested in are portable batteries for charging phones, laptops and/or other equipment. There are some events that provide electricity. If you do live events, invest in portable power packs and hotspots, to ensure you can work without relying on expensive venue electricity. It is getting even more rare for an event to have electrical outlet access. We bring our own. We recharge the battery at night at home or in a hotel room and then bring it back the next day if it is a multi-day event. That one piece of equipment has, at times, saved us hundreds and thousands of dollars because some events charge extra to be near electricity or don't guarantee that you are near an outlet at all. This is just one of the pieces of equipment that we have made investments in. What does your business need to be more desirable at events or online to become even more profitable?

It takes time to build the budget for these items, BUT you MUST re-invest in your business as it grows. You can't just eat up, spend up ALL of your profits without feeding, supporting and upgrading what you intend to feed or sustain you.

Sit down and make a list of the equipment that you would like to have. How much does it cost? Work for it. Save it and spend it wisely.

# Reflection for Review

# Phase 3
# Administrative and Financial Management

There are business owners who are great at selling, product creation and seeing a huge vision and ultimately, achieving that goal.

There are others who may be great at the big picture but struggle with the day-to-day administrative operations and financial management part of the business.

If this is NOT your strong suit, get help. Be honest with yourself. Plan and prepare to pay for the help you need and build a business that will grow with your great vision but will have the financial and administrative infrastructure and foundation to keep it alive well into the future.

# Email and List Clean-Up

Given the nature of my business, I keep all emails that are business related, client inquiry and if people have sent me manuscripts. Why? The sales cycle for my business is long. People may reach out to me; we have a conversation and then not be ready to move forward for one year or more.

Others have sent me manuscripts and their computer crashes and they ask, do you still have the email where I sent the manuscript? Yes, I do. Should I charge, probably, but I just send it as a common courtesy. Yes, I'm too nice.

Others have gone as far as receiving a contract and publishing proposal but realize that they are not ready financially or emotionally to move forward. When they come back almost 5 years later, I ask myself, what did I quote them? Is this the same book or service that they asked for 5 years ago?

Even though I have emails that are essential to my business, I have to go through and block junk senders, promo and spam emails, just to clean out and organize my inbox.

More importantly, ensure your email marketing list is organized and integrated with your website. If you have an email marketing list, you have clients or potential clients who want to stay connected to you. They can unsubscribe to your list anytime, but the other ones, you want to keep connecting with. There are times that I go through my list because people have died or unsubscribed or need to be moved to another list because they are now a signed client.

No matter what, you need to read, respond, delete emails that you don't need. I am bad about this habit and don't tackle this task but once or twice a year. I can do a search and delete them all at one time. On the other hand, I really love to organize my emails into folders of things that are extremely important to me and my business.

Finally, no matter how much junk email that you get, remember that there are potential opportunities to grow, learn and profit in those emails as well. Go through them. Grow through them. Delete the unnecessary. Respond to the essential.

# Reflection for Review

# Review Taxes Procedures

I am not a financial advisor, even though I have an accounting degree. I never worked as an accountant or a CPA. I work on my own books to organize them to get them to my CPA to prepare my books and report to the IRS. I realized a long time ago that I am NOT a paper, keep receipts type of girl. I tried for a number of the early years because my business was very small and had very little receipts to keep. As the business grew, I had to come up with another way to do it. Debit cards and credit cards were my receipts. I can easily download the information to a spreadsheet, go through the statements easier and organize it much quicker.

The majority of business owners hate this part of being in business. Paying taxes is just a part of life. Reporting how much you earned, business expenses, who you did business with and what you have left over is the very simple and basics of financial reporting.

You have to ask yourself what will work for you? Do you need a bookkeeper or a tax preparer? Do you need a CPA who understands your industry and the complex financial issues that you have going on? Prepare for it. It's expensive but worth it. Are you technology savvy and can properly use financial software after training?

Is your business making money so you are going to have to file and pay quarterly taxes or save for quarterly taxes? If so, find a CPA, find a financial advisor, find someone who can help you be organized, prepared and ready for tax season, financial advances or losses, right now and beyond.

# Reflection for Review

# Reflection for Review

# Know Your Numbers

I confess that I am NOT as consistent with this as I should be. I look at my bank account every day. I do not want to be overdrawn at all and have those fees, but at the end of the month, I do not track what I spent, what I made, what worked and what didn't. I am normally doing that at the middle of the year or at end of the year. That's too late.

Track your expenses, monthly income and how much debt that you're actually in. I am NOT a financial advisor, but I can add and multiply and know when there is a negative balance.

I am preaching to myself as much as I am writing this book for others. My new goal is to be more intentional about balancing profits between reinvestment and debt reduction. Meaning, how much debt am I really in? How much profit did I make? How much of that profit needs to go to debt instead of re-investment in some equipment, new software or some shiny object that I have seen advertised? Should I focus on marketing to the clients I have and take the profits to the debt instead of going into more debt and risk that might not get a return for months or years after the event?

That's where I am at the writing of this book. I realize that my profits are good but it mostly goes for debt and not to reinvestment, new investment or just plain savings with dividends. New terms that I've learned from the financial advisor, but I'm older and don't want to work harder BUT much smarter.

Final thing to consider. What if a very wealthy person who wanted to invest in your business asked how much debt you are in OR how much do you need to be solvent or profitable? Do you have a number? That's my prayer and the reason why I am keeping a number running in my head as well as encouraging you to have a number.

What's the number?

# Reflection for Review

# Contract and Agreement Review

Update your agreements annually. Specifically, address modern issues like AI usage requirements and "force majeure" or cancellation clauses.

Honestly, I relook, review and reword my contracts every time a situation arises. I wish I had known some issues sooner, but it hadn't come up yet. I didn't have it in the contract, but there wasn't a need yet or the issues hadn't arisen yet. My attorneys say it to me all of the time, you don't have it in a contract, so you can't get mad when somebody does something and if something happens.

When a problem arises, I change it immediately. I have my attorneys look at it, but the change can't wait for a quarterly or annual review. COVID happened in 2020.

Up until then, I hadn't had clients pass away and the families wanted me to complete the contract without paying me the balance. That had to change.

Also, I have had people take years to pay the balance because I didn't have in the contract how the long the contract would last without an adjustment or revisit to the contract. So, I didn't get my money. I'd be mad, of course, but the attorneys would say, you didn't put that in the contract. They weren't publishers. They didn't know how the sales cycle worked in publishing. Me, being new at this level of business, I didn't know to even ask. But now, I know and the contract changed.

I had to revisit the publishing journey. How many changes will I allow to the cover, the interior after the proof copy has been approved? Is there a fee for the change that late in the publishing process or not?

If someone wants to sue, where do you file, what is the state that will govern the transaction?

All types of questions may or may not arise, but as you learn more, find out what has happened with the larger companies, realize that it could happen to you, and make the change as quickly as possible.

Don't have any agreements, contracts, etc. start today. Reach out, if you need help.

## Reflection for Review

# Phase 4
# Sales, Marketing, and Relationship Building

Business is built on follow-ups, responses and customer service. Your business will rise or fall on these things.

You miss out on opportunities when you don't follow-up or follow-through. Your business will miss out on opportunities for business and/or new business when you don't respond.

Your business will become stagnant and/or die if you have poor customer service. Your logos, colors and ad copy may be beautiful, but if your customer service stinks, arrogant, rude, disrespectful and won't sacrifice to satisfy the client, you will lose.

We are human and make mistakes. No one is perfect. No matter if you are a small start-up business of less than one year or a major mogul with billions of dollars and hundreds of employees. This is what separates the three years and closed and the legacy companies. Let's go!

# Review Follow-Up System

Use January to reach out to contacts made during the previous year. A simple "Happy New Year" text or email can reignite a lead.

Better yet, whether it is after the holiday, after a meeting, after a call or after an event, follow up must occur. I normally don't miss giving a shout out during the holidays, but some events I attend get a shout out as well. Even if it is a short picture from the event, with a thank you for all who participated or didn't participate, this is a start.

No matter what season, month or day you're reading this book or going through the upcoming workbook, follow-up has been the key to my business and businesses around the world.

What emails do you need or have to reply to? What emails did you ignore and regret. What calls haven't you returned? What calls should you be returning? We all need breaks and I'm going to take a little one, but I have to still keep my business moving. I follow up by sending an email or a text that says, I'm going to be contacting you during the week of or on this day, etc. and I even put it on my calendar as a reminder. Even if the follow-up won't happen for another 1-3 months, I still put it on my calendar and I still send them a message. It is important, and I don't want to leave money on the table, so I am conscious of this effort.

Over the years, I realize that I can't remember everything like I did early on in my business. I have had to determine what that system is going to look like for follow up.

For me, if you scheduled a call with me, then you're on my email list, we have agreed on the next steps of a proposal or a session for meeting. If that happens and the client is ready to move forward, then we move forward with the publishing process for my business. But what if they are not quite ready? When do you reach out? When do you connect again?

For me, I automatically connect with anyone on my mailing list each and every month. I am intentional to send out a newsletter, inspirational, upcoming events, classes, etc., so, you hear from me automatically.

But if you have a follow-up before the newsletter, that is verified via email or text and a reminder is on my calendar. If we miss each other, we keep trying and you'll still get the newsletter. If you opt-out of the newsletter and don't respond, I realize that you are no longer interested. No hard feelings, but I went through my entire system and didn't just ignore you. I have designed, changed, revised this system for nearly 20 years.

How is that going to look for you? Do you need a more electronic system? Are you in the place and budget for a virtual assistant? Do you have agreements, contracts and proposals already available? Are you a product-only based business and don't have an online store with an email marketing system? One that reminds about the cart that hasn't been checked out or an email that notifies when things go on sale. The product-only, such as body butter, purse, jewelry, etc. are not exempt from follow-up as well. We love payments and purchases on site, but what happens after the event, after the holiday and preparing for the next event or holiday?

We have to keep going until we seal the deal and have a profitable, month, quarter and year. Follow-up matters. Let's go!

## Reflection for Review

# Reflection for Review

# Offering and Inventory Review

I have normally offered things that people have suggested or asked for. I have often offered things that I thought people wanted and it turned out they either didn't want them or wanted them and were NOT willing to pay for them.

So, what are you currently offering? Have you ever asked people, your current clients, if they would actually want or pay for what you are offering? How much are you charging? How often have you promoted it? Where are you promoting it?

I know that my core offer for my publishing company is to help you get your book edited, formatted and layout into an attractive and printable format to sell. That's it.

Helping you write the book has come out of people request. My primary business is helping someone publish their book AFTER it has already been finished and in the rough draft phase.

Over time, people have come to me with book ideas, partially finished books, books that were previously published and need to be revised. NOW, I can take you from, in my words, from your 'head to Amazon'.

But that took time to get to. I didn't work with people who hadn't finished or even written the book for the first two to three years of my business.

The first question is what is your core, main business offer? What problem are you in business to solve? What is the goal or the result of that offer? When the process is completed, what should the client have in their hands to possibly sell, enjoy or knowledge to profit from? This review of your offer can happen on a weekly, monthly, quarterly or annual basis. You always have to know what's in your hands, what's in your inventory or what's in your knowledge base that people want, need and are willing to pay for. This is the beginning of being in business. It's not the LLC, filing status, bank account, but that you have something people want and are willing to pay for.

The next question is what you currently offer, does it need to be tweaked, revised, updated or eliminated? This is ouch but must be faced and answered.

The next question is what do you need to start offering that you are unwilling to do, don't want to do or haven't asked your client base if they are willing to pay for? I have my answer already, and it pains me to even type it, but I have to face it as well.

After you have answered those questions, determine if the price that you are charging is comparable in the market place or do you need to go up or down in price? Once you decide, revise your marketing campaign and go for it. Don't worry, I have to do the same thing and do it every single year.

**Inventory**

What's in your inventory or how much inventory do you have? If somebody wanted a bulk order of one of your products, how long would it take to deliver? Do you have a discount for bulk pricing? Do you need to find a new distributor or manufacturer for your product? Do you need to hire or fire some of your staff because that product doesn't sell enough to have that large of a team? What needs to be added to your inventory that is not there now? I have finally completed a comic book for kids. They have been asking for it for years. I realize that I must work on book 2 before the spring season starts.

This book that I am working on right now is about three years behind being finished. It will get finished this time because it is necessary for my publishing AND consulting company clients.

What's missing in your inventory? Ask your clients. Check the market. Let's go!

# Reflection for Review

## Reflection for Review

# Funnel and Access Systems

How do you want people to contact you? Is there a scheduling calendar? Do they have to call you, leave a message and you call back? Do they have to reach out via social media and then you respond by direct message? Is there a website that they visit to schedule a conversation? Does that website have a lead magnet or a free download so they can get on your email list and be able to watch, follow and learn something about your work for a while until they're ready to buy or sign that contract? How will you connect with them repeatedly by newsletter, blog, etc. until then?

If you schedule a free consultation with me, you provide your name, email address and phone number. We meet on ZOOM and the only funnel or automatic emails you get from me are an automatic thank you, a reminder that we meet in a day and finally a reminder that we meet in an hour. We meet via ZOOM so I remember what you needed and I remember what I said. I do not begin a 50-email funnel after you schedule the call, to sell you something. I don't know what you need yet and you don't know whether you want to work with me or not.

On the other hand, if you schedule a paid session with me or buy something in my store, you know me, want to work me and paid to do so. That is different.

No matter how you access me, you have only signed up for my monthly newsletter or a special, holiday communication, that's it. You will be given an inspirational story, upcoming special events, classes and a reminder that if you need me, schedule a call. No pressure. No spam.

By the way, if you need more information about funnels, let's talk at www.talkwithroyston.com. Let's go!

# Reflection for Review

# Reflection for Review

# Testimonials and Receipts

Collect and record proof of your success. The young people call it 'receipts'. You need receipts for the tax department, and for the very crowded climate that we are currently in, you are going to need author, business and career receipts. What have you actually done? Who have you worked with? How many products have you sold? What events have you attended and in front of what audience?

For some people, that means everything. They do NOT buy without reviews, testimonials, referrals, word of mouth or communicating with someone who has worked with you. and after working with you, the thing that you sell, works.

I have published nearly 500 books and written 150 of my own, but there are people who still ask me for referrals. When they ask, I don't get mad, I have at least 5-

10 authors who are more than happy to give a referral. That's not boasting or arrogance, that's work. Struggle, learning, growing, changing, more study and then working on my craft, business and time management.

Who has worked with you and was happy with your product, book or business dealings? You need them to give you a reference, give a testimonial, written or on video and you need to acknowledge them in the format in which they are comfortable. Get permission, but know that if you post the testimonial on social media or that if it is posted on your website and landing page, it is promotion for them as well. It works both ways. They shout you out and you shout them out too.

Finally, don't just review and add up your receipts for the tax department, but review your receipts for doing business. It gives you the credit for being an expert in the industry and trust for the next customer. Where are your receipts?

# Reflection for Review

# Reflection for Review

# Reciprocal Partnerships

Partnership is fundamentally designed to ease the load, add value to the project. Each partner is bringing something to the table or event or product or project that one of the partners can NOT or does NOT want to do alone.

The biggest problem with partnership is first when people can't agree or each partner is supposed to bring the same thing rather than equal value.

Some partnerships are complete opposite and you don't know how they got together, but it works perfectly for the partnership and each partner. Find partners whose knowledge or audience or experience complements yours. Ensure these relationships are reciprocal rather than one-sided. One-sided partnerships that have one partner ALWAYS being the benefactor will not work. There have to be mutual benefits; otherwise, it is slavery, bondage and less than even an employer and employee relationship. At least an employee should get pay with benefits.

I highly suggest that you have a written agreement on the infrastructure, financial arrangements, non-disclosure of what is learned from the other partner as well as what happens when one partner no longer wants to be in partnership.

On the other hand, some partnerships are for referral of business to one another only. You need an agreement for that, too, and a method of knowing exactly which clients were referred. It works perfectly when it works.

Who have you partnered with? How did it go? Was it a 'one and done' or did you just partner up with the wrong person? Honestly, I ask GOD to bring people into my life who are supposed to work with me and then I ask Him for discernment to know the difference. Do you need a partner? Have qualifications, standards, and be ready.

# Reflection for Review

# Reflection for Review

# Phase 5
# Growth and Professional Development

You can't grow if you don't learn, study and change. That's my perspective and I am sticking with it.

I don't like change and enjoy routine, but when it no longer works, it doesn't work. Rather than walk in pride, be stubborn and remain loyal to something that NO LONGER works, I have to search out the information, software, program or new strategy I need, learn it and execute.

But, first things first, I have to work on me, to be open, receptive and willing to schedule the time to learn something and pivot in a different direction.

Wanting to scale or expand by staying in the same place, doing the same old thing and/or haven't learned anything new that would at least improve what works, will not work.

Let's study to know, then change to grow.

# Mentor, Coaching and/or Consultant

Identify if you need a business coach, financial advisor, writing coach, or even a therapist to handle the emotional toll of entrepreneurship.

The right mentor or a coach or a consultant in your business can help guide you and help you determine the best strategies, methods and directions to take you and your business. Is the next level really right for you? If so, what does the next level look like for you compared to someone else in that same business or industry?

To get to the next level, you must see who is already where you are trying to go and has been where you are right now. How did they get from where you are to where they are? Are they willing to show, tell and direct you? What is their work ethic like? What is their method of consulting? Show me or tell me or a mixture of both? You have to be honest with yourself and determine if you easily connect with people or do you need time? It might be the coach or consultant or it might be you and your personality who is stalling or stopping progress.

Everybody doesn't connect with everybody, and I get that. Secondly, there is a coach for you, but are you open to it? Do you take correction or guidance well? If they don't agree with you, do you walk away even if they have been very successful at how they have done it? Absolutely, get references or referrals, but be sure to know why this or that person didn't work for you. Let me tell you something: if everyone you work with is not this or that, I mean everybody, and you can't seem to work with anybody, I referred or not??!! Then check the man in the mirror, it might be you.

Remember, there are some things that you can only learn from someone who has been there. The videos, courses, mastermind and books don't tell you everything.

Your situation may be customized and you may have specific needs that aren't in the book. You may need a guide to guide you through the process like a five-year-old across the busy street. Be aware of that and acknowledge that as well.

Next, once you find someone you think will be a good fit, respect the expert. You may not agree with everything they say or their methods, but hear them out, especially if you paid for the course and their time.

Respect their time.

Arrive on time.

Complete the assignment and show up prepared. You can't get out of something that you didn't put in.

You can move alone, but you can move faster with the information and a person pointing and leading the way. It is sometimes safer that way, and hopefully, you make less mistakes with a mentor, coach and consultant. You don't have to agree or do what they say, but at least you have the information to make the decision that works for you.

As you can tell, I'm pretty thorough and not a gatekeeper. I don't like gatekeepers and strive not to be one, especially if someone is a paid client. I probably over teach, instruct and give more information than others do because I want to sleep at night and must go to heaven in the end.

Finally, remember that you're working with a person with feelings. There may be coaches who do get jealous and then, for me, it is time to go. There may be a mentor who is not comfortable in their own skin and would like to go back some years and relive some things that they didn't get to do but striving to do it through you. It's time to go then too.

When you do find that mentor, coach or consultant, who wants you to win almost more than you do, hold them with the highest respect, do NOT take advantage, and always remember them no matter where life takes you. These people are rare and may be partially angelic.

# Reflection for Review

# Professional Development

As a retired educator, I remember that it was a requirement for me to have 24 hours of professional development to maintain my certification to keep my job as a teacher. Even the year that I was planning to retire, the summer before, I still had to drive to the schools, go through the halls, find the classrooms, sign in, electronically or on paper and then sit down just like a student, to learn what was taught to be able to get the hours I needed for the year. I had to turn in proof or receipts that I had attended the 24 hours at the beginning of the school year before the first day of school. It was mandatory. Throughout the year, I would send the list of technology classes to the teachers who struggled with technology. I didn't want them to be in the same, struggling place next year that they were in this year. As the technology coordinator for the building, it made my job a lot easier.

Amazingly enough, some of the skills I learned back then have been very helpful and critical to my business today. If I needed it then, I still need it in my business today.

With that said, commit to learning a new skill every day, month, quarter or year. Whether through YouTube, your local library, or paid courses, stay current with industry trends so you aren't paying for things you don't understand or need. There may be an easier, cheaper and faster way to do things. But if you don't find new ways, new systems and new technology, you'll be spending more time doing things the same way, when there could be a more modern and efficient way. Keep up. Reach out. Learn more to help you go up faster.

# Reflection for Review

# Reflection for Review

# New Product/Service Creation

What does your audience keep asking you for? What do they want? If they say they want it, ask them how much they are willing to pay for it. If they tell you and it works for you, do it.

I mentioned earlier about the comic book. My pride wouldn't let me write it before because I was trying to force reluctant readers to read chapter books. Some had their parents buy the books hesitantly, but I knew deep down they didn't want to read the book. Hopefully, it was interesting enough to keep their attention, but I knew that they really wanted a comic book type book. Interesting story, fewer pages and more visual.

I got encouragement from other comic book authors, illustrators and graphic designers. They all said, "Julia, you can do it!" My husband was willing to help me and not make me feel bad or look stupid, so we did it together. He was my technical and visual consultant. I had never done it before, but I know that there is an audience waiting on this book and this product to come from this story and ME! I have even sent an unedited version to the elementary school that wants it the most. It's not done, but I had to get them excited for it.

What has your audience been asking you for? Stop procrastinating and give them what they want. Listen to your audience. If people are asking for a specific product (like a book, workbook, journal, or even a comic book), get started outlining and writing it. If they want an accompanying, or just complementing, product to your product, find it and charge them. What's new? Create, Design, Package and Sell it.

# Reflection for Review

# Reflection for Review

# Team Building

I have to confess that I enjoy being a solopreneur or business owner. I love the solo creative and execution process, but I can only do so much alone. I hire editors, graphics people, virtual assistants and coaches to help me be a better business owner.

I don't have an actual hired W-2 employee because I don't want to deal with someone each and every day, but I have people whom I can call when there is a project too large or that would benefit both of us.

I don't want to spend or try to save for a budget to hire more people. I want to outsource with other businesses to help them grow their businesses while I grow and manage mine. Now, I do know how to call in help when I get overwhelmed or if there is too much for me. Which I love doing, but I have got to face the facts and empower the team that I am working with and building so that they can be their best as well. I am used to working alone and having the instructions in my head, but you can't have it in your head when working with someone else. You need videos, policies and procedures, instructions via written and visual, to properly train the team to be the best that they can be and, ultimately, be the best for what you and your brand need and have to have to stay in business.

Evaluate if you have outgrown being a "solopreneur". Besides the money that is necessary to afford to expand your team, you may have to pay for a coach to coach you on how to lead, train, develop and turn loose a team to work independently of you and not micromanage them to burn out and frustration. Build you first. Then build the team. Then let the team build the brand.

Who is on your team?

# Reflection for Review

# Reflection for Review

# Mission and Boundary Check

Whether it is once a year, every month or every week, some new people may have stumbled upon your social media page or website OR, more importantly, people who have been following you or watching you for a while, no longer remember what you do, how long you have been doing it, what you NOW offer compared to what you offered when they first met you. Re-introduce yourself to them and your brand.

When I first started my business nearly 20 years ago, I had 2 clients. Myself and one other person. I was proud to just be asked and paid to publish someone else's book. That was it, the end of story, but that was in 2007. A long way from 1 other client besides myself, I am now nearly 400 clients deep, 500 books published, helping people write their own books, start their own publishing companies and businesses surrounding and based on their books. Consulting, internet radio show host, podcaster, non-profit founder and more to come if I keep living. Not to mention, most people know me as an author and publisher and have never heard me sing or know that I have recorded three music CDs. Did you know that? Let me re-introduce you to me and my brands.

Next, reconfirm what your brand stands for. Emphasize how you got into business, why you started a business and how things have been along the way. Not the whole story, but some highs and lows of your journey. It is empowering, inspiring and if some people can see it, they can be it too.

Next, you may have to re-adjust, remind people about the reposition of your boundaries, your limitations and your goals and objectives. I don't suggest a social media, YouTube or website rant. Just make sure that when you're asked about what you will and will not do, you make it nice and clear about what your boundaries are. What do your products do for people and how do they make their lives better? How do your services make the future look brighter, and what part will it play in their legacy as well as your own? Remind people of how far you have come, how many years you've been in your 'game' and where you are headed into the future. Don't give all of the dreams, hopes and plans until the deal is finished, but give them enough to want to meet you and know more.

You also have to have boundaries for outsiders. You have to know who you will and won't work with in your mind. You need discernment when it comes to speaking with people versus reading their emails or what is on paper. For me, I have to talk to you or see you via ZOOM. I have to hear your heart and then still pray to God to make sure that I don't get taken advantage of. You have to have your own ethics and personal moral boundaries. At times, you may have to say "no" to very profitable opportunities if it crosses the line.

Write it down and know the expectations for the client and the expectation that you have for yourself. What you can and cannot do, or more importantly, even if you can do it, will you or will you NOT do it?

How do you want to be contacted in the reintroduction? Back in the day, it didn't matter if you called on the phone, texted, in-boxed or emailed me, I would respond. Today, I can text, inbox or email you back pretty quickly, but calling on the phone is hard because I don't know where I'll be and what I'll be doing at any given time. It's best to schedule a conversation at www.talkwithroyston.com. I mentioned it in an earlier chapter about access systems but it is becoming more important now than ever. With an appointment, you have my full and undistracted attention.

Finally, with the re-introductions and boundaries, consider writing blog posts, articles, a monthly or quarterly newsletter or have a commemorative magazine that talks about your journey, how to best work with you and how to access your website, store and other product and services.

Who needed you back then may be different from who wants to work with you now. Revisit and restate your mission, put up the boundaries and preserve your peace, profits and prosperity.

## Reflection for Review

# Reflection for Review

# Reflection for Review

# About the Author

Julia Royston spends her days doing what she loves, writing, publishing, speaking about her why and motto, "Helping You Get Your Message to the Masses, Turn Your Words into Wealth and Be a Book Business Boss." Julia is the author of 150+ books, published 500+, recorded 3 music CDs and coached others to be published authors and business owners. She is the owner of five companies, a non-profit organization and the editor of the Book Business Boss Magazine.

To stay connected with Julia, visit www.juliaakroyston.com.

Social Media

Facebook, Instagram, LinkedIn, TikTok and Threads - @juliaaroyston

YouTube - @bkroystonpublishing @bookbusinessboss

# Other Books by This Author

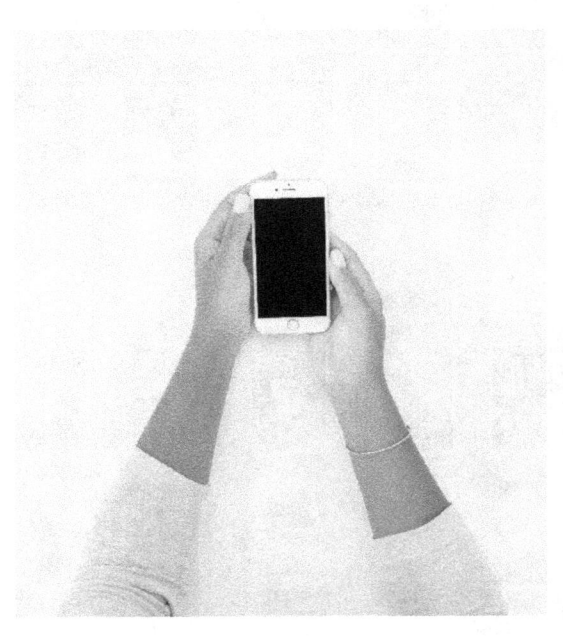

www.ingramcontent.com/pod-product-compliance
Lightning Source LLC
Chambersburg PA
CBHW071215160426
43196CB00012B/2306